Behind a Yellow Yak

Written by Mario Scavatto

Illustrated by Patrick Joseph

Where can you hide a yellow yo-yo?

2

Where can you hide a yellow yam?

Where can you hide a yellow car?

4

Where can you hide a yellow truck?

Where can you hide a yellow house?

Where can you hide a yellow barn?

Behind a yellow yak.